Credits

Cover, © iStockphoto/Thinkstock; 2–3, © Eric Isselee/Shutterstock; 4, © patpitchaya/Shutterstock; 5, © Dmitry Kovtun/Shutterstock; 6, © Eric Isselee/Shutterstock; 7, © Martin Valigursky/Shutterstock; 9, © GunnerL/Shutterstock; 10, © Covenant/Shutterstock; 11, © Gerard Lacz/age fotostock/Superstock; 12, © Gerard Lacz/age fotostock/Superstock; 13, © Kitch Bain/Shutterstock; 14, © Jurgen & Christine Sohns/FLPA; 15, © D. Parer & E. Parer-Cook/Ardea; 16, © Roland Seitre/Nature Picture Library; 17, © Bruce & Jan Lichtenberger/Superstock; 18, © John Carnemolla/Shutterstock; 19, © Gerard Lacz/FLPA; 20, © Janelle Lugge/Shutterstock; 21, © worldswildlifewonders/Shutterstock; 22, © Jurgen & Christine Sohns/FLPA, © D. Parer & E. Parer-Cook/Ardea, © Bruce & Jan Lichtenberger/Superstock, © Gerard Lacz/FLPA, and © GunnerL/Shutterstock; 23TL, © Mopic/Shutterstock; 23TC, © RTImages/Shutterstock; 23TR, © Susan Flashman/Shutterstock; 23BL, © D. Parer & E. Parer-Cook/Ardea; 23BC, © Jurgen & Christine Sohns/FLPA; 23BR, © Bruce Lichtenberger/Getty Images; 24, © Susan Flashman/Shutterstock, © Cynthia Kidwell/Shutterstock, and © Barbara Dobner.

Publisher: Kenn Goin
Creative Director: Spencer Brinker
Design: Emma Randall
Editor: Mark J. Sachner
Photo Researcher: Ruby Tuesday Books Ltd

Library of Congress Cataloging-in-Publication Data

Phillips, Dee, 1967-
  Koala / by Dee Phillips.
    p. cm. — (Treed: animal life in the trees)
  Includes bibliographical references and index.
  ISBN-13: 978-1-61772-916-4 (library binding)
  ISBN-10: 1-61772-916-7 (library binding)
  1. Koala—Juvenile literature. 2. Koala—Behavior—Juvenile literature. I. Title.
  QL737.M384P464 2014
  599.2'5—dc23
                    2013005570

For more information, write to Bearport Publishing Company, Inc., 45 West 21st Street, Suite 3B, New York, New York 10010. Printed in the United States of America.

10 9 8 7 6 5 4 3 2 1

Contents

A Gum Tree Home

It's a hot, sunny afternoon in a gum tree forest.

In the branches of a tall tree, a furry gray animal is taking a nap.

The sleepy animal is a koala.

Koalas spend nearly all their time in treetops.

They eat, sleep, and even raise their babies high above the ground.

gum tree forest

Check Out a Koala

A koala's treetop home doesn't give it much protection from the weather.

Luckily, koalas have thick fur.

On cold days, the koala's fur keeps the animal warm.

On hot days, the fur protects the animal's skin from the sun.

A koala's fur also acts like a raincoat.

On rainy days, it keeps the animal's body dry.

thick fur

An adult koala's body is about 30 inches (76 cm) long from its nose to its bottom. It weighs between 11 and 26 pounds (5 and 12 kg).

Life in the Forest

Koalas live in gum tree forests in Australia.

Every koala lives in a part of the forest called its **home range**.

A home range may be just a few trees or an area the size of several football fields.

A koala's home range often overlaps with the ranges of other koalas.

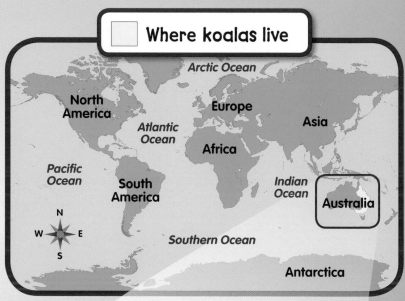

Where koalas live

Arctic Ocean

North America

Europe

Asia

Atlantic Ocean

Africa

Pacific Ocean

South America

Indian Ocean

Australia

N
W   E
S

Southern Ocean

Antarctica

Australia

Koalas are very good at climbing and moving around in trees. What parts of their bodies do you think help them do this?

Moving Through the Forest

To move through the forest, koalas often leap from tree to tree.

They also walk along branches, gripping them with their toes and long claws.

If koalas can't reach a new tree, they climb down to the ground.

Then they walk to the next tree and climb up its trunk.

claws

tree trunk

If koalas spend most of their time in trees, what do you think they eat and drink?

a koala leaping to reach a new tree

When it's time to sleep, a koala gets comfortable on a branch and dozes off.

11

Leafy Meals

There's not much for a koala to eat in a gum tree—except leaves.

Every day, an adult koala eats just over a pound (453 g) of leaves.

The oil in the leaves is poisonous to most animals but not to koalas.

Koalas have special **bacteria** in their stomachs.

The bacteria break down the poison so it doesn't hurt the koalas.

The pouch is here.

A female koala has a pocket-like **pouch** on the outside of her belly. What do you think she uses this pouch for?

Koalas get most of the water they need by eating gum tree leaves. Each juicy leaf has a little water inside it. Koalas also swallow raindrops and **dew** that collect on the leaves.

gum tree leaf

A Baby Koala

Between August and December, male and female koalas meet up to **mate**.

About 35 days later, a female koala gives birth to a baby called a joey.

When it's born, the joey is only the size of a jellybean!

The baby koala has no fur or ears, and its eyes are closed.

The tiny joey climbs into a warm pouch on its mother's belly.

Safe inside, it drinks milk from its mother's body.

Koalas make a noise called a bellow. It sounds like a snore followed by a burp. Males often make this noise to tell females they want to mate.

a five-day-old joey inside its mother's pouch

Gum Tree Baby

By the time it's six months old, a joey's eyes have opened.

Its fur and ears have also grown.

The joey still drinks milk, but it also eats leaves and a food called pap.

Pap is a special type of mother koala poop!

A mother koala's body turns gum tree leaves into pap that the joey licks from her body.

a 12-week-old joey inside its mother's pouch

Koalas belong to a group of animals called **marsupials**. All marsupials give birth to tiny babies that are not fully formed. A marsupial baby finishes growing inside its mother's pouch, instead of inside her body.

mother koala

a six-month-old joey looking out of its mother's pouch

What other animals can you think of that are marsupials and carry their babies in pouches?
(The answer is on page 24.)

A Piggyback Ride

At about nine months old, a joey weighs around two pounds (1 kg).

The baby koala can no longer fit inside its mother's pouch.

Instead, the joey rides through the gum trees on its mother's back.

sleeping koala

Gum tree leaves don't give koalas much energy to do things. As a result, koalas are only awake about four hours each day. They sleep during the other twenty hours.

one-year-old joey

mother koala

Off Into the Forest

At about 18 months old, a joey is ready to leave its mother.

The young koala climbs through the trees to find its own home range.

Once in its home range, it spends its time sleeping and munching on gum tree leaves.

Koalas live for about 8 to 15 years.

adult female koala

joey

Scientists who study koalas have to search for them in gum tree forests. If you were looking for koalas, what clues would tell you they were nearby?

(The answer is on page 24.)

Science Lab

Draw a Koala's Life Cycle

The different stages of an animal's life are known as its life cycle.

The diagram on this page shows the life cycle of a koala.

Use the photographs in this book to help you draw and label a koala's life cycle.

How to Draw a Koala

You can draw a koala's head, ears, body, and feet using circles and ovals.

A male and female koala mate.

A jellybean-size joey is born and lives in its mother's pouch.

A Koala's Life Cycle

At l8 months old, a koala leaves its mother.

At nine months old, the joey rides on its mother's back.

At six months old, the joey looks out of the pouch.

Science Words

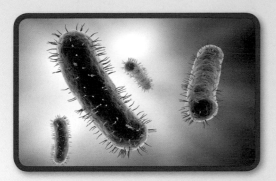

bacteria (bak-TIHR-ee-uh) tiny living things that can only be seen with a microscope; some bacteria are helpful, while others can cause disease

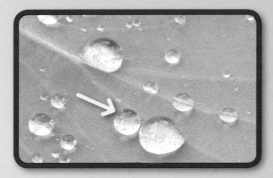

dew (DOO) water in the air that collects on things that are outside

home range (HOHM RAYNJ) the area where an animal lives and finds its food

marsupials (mar-SOO-pee-uhlz) a group of animals in which the young are raised in pouches on the mothers' bellies

mate (MAYT) to come together in order to have young

pouch (POUCH) a pocket-like part of a mother koala's belly used to carry her young

Index

Read More

Bodden, Valerie. *Koalas (Amazing Animals).* Mankato, MN: Creative Education (2009).

Kras, Sara Louise. *Koalas (Australian Animals).* Mankato, MN: Capstone (2010).

Learn More Online

To learn more about koalas, visit **www.bearportpublishing.com/Treed**

About the Author

Dee Phillips lives near the ocean on the southwest coast of England. She develops and writes nonfiction and fiction books for children of all ages.

Answers

Page 17: Kangaroos, wallabies, wombats, Tasmanian devils, and opossums are all marsupials and carry their babies in pouches.

Page 21: If you are searching for koalas:
- Listen for koala bellows.
- Look for claw marks on tree trunks.
- Look for koala poop on the ground.

wallaby

opossum

koala claw marks

koala poop